# Multitask with JARVIS & DAD

Book 1

Written by Jashon Sykes

Illustrated by Richard Peter David

**Learnwithjarvis.com**

Copyright 2018

ISBN: 978-1-7322430-0-2

Printed in the United States

**#Multitaskwithjarvis&dad**

**#Learnwithjarvis**

COLOSSAL
INTEGRATIONS

*This Book*
***Belongs to:***

COLOSSAL
INTEGRATIONS

"Dad, wake-up! It's time to go to work and I have to go to school!"

Dad says, "Jarvis, it's the weekend." "The weekend?!" Jarvis shouts. "So I don't have school today? Yes!"

With a soft voice Dad says, "Remember Jarvis, no school on the weekends. How about today we have a Dad-and-Son playdate?" Jarvis is now overly excited, "a Dad-and-Son playdate? Yes!"

4

Jarvis zooms down the stair-rail and into the laundry room.

"Wahoo," Jarvis shouts! Jarvis was going so fast that he almost fell off the side of the stair-rail!

In the laundry room, Jarvis grabs his hat, the leash for Brutis, gloves, a sponge, wash bucket, a football, and his basketball.

Jarvis zooms back upstairs.

Jarvis runs back into Dad's room and excitedly says, "Dad, let's walk Brutis. Then, we can shoot some hoops, cut the grass, wash the car, and play catch!"

Dad says, "OK Jarvis, make sure your room is clean, and let's brush our teeth before we go outside."

While brushing their teeth, Jarvis tries to copy his Dad's every move. Jarvis watches his Dad in the mirror and brushes his tongue like him.

Jarvis then tries to watch TV while putting on his shorts just like his Dad, but Jarvis seems to have a hard time doing both.

"Dad, I can't do it! How come you can do everything and I can't?" Jarvis asks.

Dad chuckles as he kneels down on one knee. Dad puts his hand on Jarvis's shoulder an says, "Jarvis, we're Multitaskers, and remember Jarvis, we don't say I can't. We also don't give excuses, we just have to keep trying, and practice at the things we want t be good at." "Ok you're right, but Dad, Multitaskers? What is a Multitasker?" Jarvis a

"Jarvis, before I tell you what a Multitasker is, you must first put your thinking cap on," Dad says.

Jarvis is excited to learn what a Multitasker is. Jarvis says, "It's on Dad, now tell me! Tell me!"

"Ok, a Multitasker is someone who can do many things at one time." Dad says.

"Many things at one time?" Jarvis asks, "Hmm, Ok, I got it! So a Multitasker is a person who can eat ice cream, watch cartoons, and play ball at the same time, right?"

12

With a soft laugh, Dad says, "That is correct, Jarvis; you'll be doing many things at one time. Now Son, let's walk Brutis to the park and shoot some hoops."

While walking to the park, Jarvis copies his Dad's every move. Dad reminds Jarvis that adults should always walk closest to the street on the side walk. They do this to avoid anger or any accidents.

At the park, Jarvis and Dad play a game of basketball.

After their game, Dad shows Jarvis a trick with the ball and spins it on his finger.

"Wow Dad, that's so cool! I wish I could do that," Jarvis says. "Well Son, I'm going to make your wish come true. Give me your finger," says Dad.

"I'm doing it! I'm doing it Dad!"
Jarvis shouts.

"Yes you are," Dad says. "Now let's head home so we can wash the car, cut the grass, and play catch."

At home, Jarvis and Dad Multitask.
They cut the grass, wash the car, and play catch
at the same time.

"Great throw Jarvis," Dad shouts.

While playing catch with Dad, Jarvis seems to be watering down more than just the car. He wets Brutis too!

Dad and Jarvis work together to dry off the car, and Brutis.

"Nice job, Jarvis!" Dad replies. "The car looks brand new; give me five son! Great Multitasking, wouldn't you say?"

"Great Multitasking is right." Jarvis replies, "So Dad, what's next, ice cream and cartoons?" Dad laughs, "No son, let's try showers and a nap."

Aww, nap time? I took a shower last night. Our day just just got started Dad." Jarvis whines. "Remember Jarvis, even when you don't like what Dad is saying, you still have to be a good listener and do as you're told."

Dad reminds Jarvis that we need to use our 2's more than our 1's. Dad explains to Jarvis that we have 2 ears, 2 eyes, and only 1 mouth for a reason. Dad explains to Jarvis that we should listen and use our eyes more than we talk. We can learn when we're listening and use our eyes. We do not learn things when we are talking.

While Jarvis is asleep, Dad scoops his favorite ice cream and turns on cartoons so they are ready when he wakes up.

When you are having fun, the days go fast.

The word we learned today was...Multitask.

"Did you brush your teeth? Did you clean your room?" Dad asked.

Jarvis is reminded this is an everyday task.

Jarvis washed the car, while Dad cut the grass.

Together as a team, they finished the job fast!

Even Brutis had a blast!

Jarvis's short nap did not last,

he wants ice cream while watching cartoons so he can...Multitask!

# Lessons Learned with Jarvis:

- Make sure your room is clean

- Brush your teeth before you go outside

- Don't say I can't

- Don't give excuses

- Keep trying

- Practice at the things you want to be good at

- Multitask – To do many things at one time

- Be a good listener

- Adults should always walk closest to the street on the side walk

- Dream Big

- Listen and use your eyes more than you talk. You do not learn things when you are talking